A Holy Card Prayer Book II

A Compilation of Saints and Holy People

Text
Leaflet Missal Company Staff

Artist
Anna May McCallum

The Leaflet Missal Company
976 West Minnehaha Avenue Saint Paul, Minnesota 55104

Printed in U.S.A.

Nihil Obstat:

Richard J. Schuler
Censor Deputatus

Imprimatur:

✢ John R. Roach, D.D.
Archbishop of St. Paul and Minneapolis

Copyright © The Leaflet Missal Company

All rights reserved. No part of this book may be reproduced or transmitted in any form or by any means, electronic or mechanical, including photo-copying, recording or by any information storage and retrieval system, without permission in writing from the Publisher.

ISBN: 1-885845-01-4

Published, printed and bound in U.S.A.

THE LEAFLET MISSAL COMPANY
976 W. Minnehaha Ave.
St. Paul, MN 55104

Dedication

We dedicate this book to the Good Shepherd Who lays down His life for His sheep and feeds them with His Body and Blood that they will follow the voice of His word and have eternal life in the pasture of heaven.

Table of Contents

The Annunciation	3	St. Lawrence	61
Blessed Josephine Bakhita	5	The Little Flower	63
St. Bridget of Sweden	7	St. Louis de Montfort	65
Our Lady of Mount Carmel	9	Blessed Margaret Castello	67
St. Catherine Labouré	11	St. Margaret Clitherow	69
St. Catherine of Siena; St. Rose	13	St. Mark	71
St. Charles Borromeo; St. Aloysius	15	Martha and Mary	73
The Child Jesus	17	Louis and Zélie Martin	75
Christ the King	19	Mother Angelica	77
St. Clare of Assisi	21	Mother of Sorrows	79
David and Goliath	23	Mother Teresa	81
The Death of Joseph	25	St. Nicholas	83
St. Dominic	27	St. Paul Miki and Companions	85
The Four Evangelists	29	St. Philip Neri	87
The Message of Fátima	31	St. Philomena	89
Blessed Faustina Kowalska	33	The Poor Souls in Purgatory	91
St. Francis de Sales; St. Jane	35	Pope John Paul II	93
Blessed Gianna Beretta Molla	37	The Presentation of the Child Jesus	95
The Good Shepherd	39	Queen of Heaven and Earth	97
St. Hermenegild	41	St. Raphael and Tobias	99
"I am the Resurrection"	43	St. Rita of Cascia	101
Blessed Imelda	45	Archbishop Fulton J. Sheen	103
St. Jerome	47	St. Stephen	105
Jesus is Laid in the Tomb	49	St. Teresa of Ávila	107
St. Joan of Arc	51	Blessed Teresa Benedicta	109
St. John the Baptist	53	St. Thomas Aquinas	111
St. John Neumann	55	The Unborn Child	113
Blessed Juan Diego	57	St. Vincent de Paul	115
King David	59		

The Annunciation

THE ANNUNCIATION OF THE BLESSED VIRGIN MARY is the announcement from the angel Gabriel to Mary that she, who was full of grace, was chosen to be the Mother of God. Mary responds to God's proposal of the mystery of the Incarnation and, in the name of all humanity, says, "behold the handmaid of the Lord; be it done unto me according to Thy word." Through her free consent, God the Son descends from heaven to earth to dwell in the incorruptible paradise of her Immaculate Heart. At the message of the angel, she becomes the Mother of God made man, He Who is true God and true Man, and unconditionally accepts the gift of divine motherhood for the salvation of the world. Through the power of the Holy Spirit, she becomes the new ark of the covenant revealing God's glory and contains the true Manna of heaven, the divine Holy of Holies in the sanctuary of her radiant Heart. Mary's faith undid Eve's rejection of the word of God and conceived the sinless Lamb of God that made her the fruitful bride of God that would bring forth sons and daughters who are born through the redeeming grace of God.

The Angelus

V. The angel of the Lord declared unto Mary. *R.* And she conceived of the Holy Spirit. Hail Mary, etc. *V.* Behold the handmaid of the Lord. *R.* Be it done unto me according to thy word. Hail Mary, etc. *V.* And the Word was made Flesh. *R.* And dwelt among us. Hail Mary, etc. *V.* Pray for us, O holy Mother of God. *R.* That we may be made worthy of the promises of Christ.

Let us Pray:

Pour forth, we beseech Thee, O Lord, Thy grace into our hearts, that we to whom the Incarnation of Christ, Thy Son, was made known by the message of an angel, may by His Passion and Cross, be brought to the glory of His Resurrection. Through the same Christ our Lord. Amen.

Blessed Josephine Bakhita, pray for us!

Blessed Josephine Bakhita

JOSEPHINE BAKHITA was born in 1869 in the area of Darfur in the Sudan. She had three brothers and four sisters. At the age of nine, she was kidnapped and sold to slave merchants, never to see her family again. Her captors named her Bakhita, meaning "lucky one." She was moved with other slaves in walking caravans across desert and forest land, having a padlocked chain around her neck. She worked for an Arabian chief, but after disappointing him, she was beaten and sold to a Turkish general, serving him for three years and receiving a daily punishment. She was scourged by his soldiers and once cruelly tattooed. She was then sold to an Italian master in Khartoum who sent her to Italy to be a nursemaid. An administrator of her master in Venice helped her to enter a boarding school run by the Canossian sisters where she came to know "God whom I had experienced in my soul since childhood without knowing Who He was." She took instructions in the Catholic faith, and, "with a joy that only the angels could describe," was baptized with the name of Josephine, confirmed and received her First Holy Communion from the Cardinal Patriarch of Venice on Jan. 9, 1890. She was accepted into the religious life by Cardinal Giuseppe Sarto, the future St. Pius X, and became a Canossian Daughter of Charity on Dec. 8, 1896. She died on Feb. 8, 1947 and was beatified by Pope John Paul II on May 17, 1992, who honored her on her own soil during his pastoral visit to Khartoum on Feb. 10, 1993.

Prayer to Blessed Josephine

God the Father of Mercy, You have given us the splendid gift of Blessed Josephine Bakhita, a shining example of the spirit of the beatitudes. Through her intercession may we obey You with a happy heart, and reach out to all people to bring them the light of faith, that we may belong to You alone. Through Christ our Lord. Amen.

St. Bridget of Sweden

BRIDGET was born in 1303 to a wealthy Swedish family. In obedience to the wishes of her father, she was married at the age of fourteen to a prince. She raised eight children, one of whom became St. Catherine of Sweden. After twenty-eight years of marriage, her husband died and she relinquished her title of princess and founded an order devoted to the Most Holy Savior. She led pilgrimages to Rome and the Holy Land out of her love for the sufferings of Christ. She reformed monasteries and worked to restore the papal throne to Rome. On numerous occasions, she denounced the evil ways of public officials. Bridget received prophetic insights and visions and wrote fifteen magnificent prayers on the Passion of Jesus. She said that Jesus was the "mirror of eternal splendor...the treasure of every real good and every joy." She prayed that Christ's sufferings "be renewed in my soul." She died in Rome in 1373 and was canonized in 1391. She is the patroness of Sweden.

St. Bridget, Widow

O Lord our God, Who revealed through Thy Son heavenly messages to Thy servant Bridget, grant that we, by her intercession, may renounce the comforts of the world to follow Thy Son's Word and glory in His Cross and so come to the full revelation of Thy glory in heaven. Through Christ our Lord. Amen.

Prayer to St. Bridget

O St. Bridget, by your devotion to the Passion and Death of Jesus Christ, may I resist the world, the flesh and the devil that the fruits of His sufferings may be renewed in my soul and I will live for God and have true contrition and remission of all my sins. In the name of Jesus Christ the Lord. Amen.

Our Lady of Mount Carmel

OUR LADY OF MOUNT CARMEL is the patronal feast of Carmelites that is celebrated on July 16. She appeared to St. Simon Stock, a Carmelite, on July 16, 1251, holding in her hand a Brown Scapular, and promised him that those who wear it shall not suffer eternal fire. According to tradition, those who faithfully wear the Brown Scapular, observe chastity according to their state in life and recite daily her Little Office or fulfill an approved Marian practice will be released from Purgatory the first Saturday after their death. The Brown Scapular is blessed with many indulgences and is a sign that we belong to Mary who is perfectly consecrated to the will of God. She is prefigured on Mount Carmel by the cloud which poured forth a bountiful rain, a sign of sanctifying grace that would descend to earth in the incarnation of Eternal Wisdom. She is the garden and vine of God through which God fulfills His covenant with man that was renewed on Mount Carmel after Elijah converted the prophets of Baal to belief in the one true God with fire from heaven. Mary is an icon of divine grace, *gratia plena*, that brings forth Divine Wisdom, the new mountain of contemplation. At Fátima in 1917, she appeared as Our Lady of Mount Carmel in the miracle of the sun, confirming devotion to the Brown Scapular that clothes us with her virtues. She is the spiritual mother of mankind who forms the life of Jesus in us that we may love God as she loves Him in her Immaculate Heart.

Prayer to Our Lady of Mount Carmel

O most blessed and immaculate Virgin, ornament and beauty of Mount Carmel, thou who beholdest with thy special kindness those who wear thy blessed Scapular, look lovingly upon me, and cover me with the mantle of thy motherly protection. Fortify my weakness with thy power, enlighten the darkness of my understanding with thy wisdom, increase Faith, Hope and Charity in me, adorn my soul with the graces and virtues that will make me pleasing to thee and thy divine Son. Assist me during my life, and console me at the hour of my death and present me to the most blessed Trinity as thy devoted servant, to praise and bless thee in heaven forever. Amen.

St. Catherine Labouré

CATHERINE LABOURÉ was born in Fain-les-Moutiers, France in 1806. When she was young, her mother died and she cared for the family without attending school. She desired to become a nun to serve the elderly and the sick. In 1830 she entered the Daughters of Charity founded by St. Vincent de Paul. That same year, her guardian angel led her to the convent chapel for the first of three apparitions of Our Lady. On the third visit, Our Lady told her to have a medal made in honor of the Immaculate Conception with the words "O Mary, conceived without sin, pray for us who have recourse to thee" on the frontside and an image of Hearts of Jesus and Mary on the back. In 1832, the Archbishop of Paris permitted the making of the medal and in 1836 he approved the apparitions. The medal, known as the Miraculous Medal, spread throughout the world and became instrumental in obtaining cures, conversions and graces for "persons who wear it with confidence." Until her death in 1876, St. Catherine did not reveal her visions to anyone except her confessor and continued to serve the infirm in a hospice. She was canonized in 1947 and her body has remained incorrupt. The devotion of the Miraculous Medal is extensively promoted by members of the Legion of Mary.

The Miraculous Medal

O Lord Jesus Christ, Who preserved Thy Mother, the Blessed Virgin Mary free from the stain of sin at the moment of her conception and was pleased that she should shine with countless miracles of grace, grant that through her patronage we may obtain the joy of everlasting life. Amen.

St. Catherine Labouré

Lord our God, Who granted unto St. Catherine a vision of the Immaculate Virgin Mary, Thy Mother, we ask Thee after the example of blessed Catherine for a tender devotion to Thy holy Mother that we may enjoy the grace of eternal life. Amen.

St. Catherine of Siena; St. Rose

CATHERINE BENINCASA was born in Siena, Italy in 1347, the youngest of twenty-five children in her family. At age six, she received a vision of Jesus. After she became a third order Dominican at age eighteen, she lived at home and for three years spoke only to God and her confessor. She converted sinners, nursed the sick and worked miracles for the poor. When she fasted, her only food was Holy Communion. She supported the Crusades and convinced the pope to return the papal throne to Rome. She wrote a book, the *Dialogue*, about her mystical experiences and received the invisible stigmata in 1375. She died in 1380, was canonized in 1461 and became a Doctor of the Church in 1970. St. Rose, born in 1586 in Lima, Peru, was named Rose after her mother saw a rose drooping over her crib. She became a third order Dominican, received the invisible stigmata and was devoted to the Passion of Christ, praying and sacrificing for sinners. She lived in a small hut in her father's garden where Jesus appeared to her. Her head was crowned with thorns over which she wore a crown of roses. She died in 1617 and was canonized the first American saint in 1671.

St. Catherine of Siena

Most Holy Spirit, source of unity in the Blessed Trinity, through the prayers of St. Catherine, may the Church always be a sign of unity in faith and morals under the leadership of the Holy Father, the divinely chosen authority who speaks in the name of Jesus Christ. Who with the Father and the Son lives and reigns forever. Amen.

St. Rose of Lima

Almighty God, Who bestows bountiful gifts, and willed that St. Rose, bedewed with heavenly gifts, should blossom forth as a lovely flower of virginity and patience, may we follow her way and become a sweet savor of Christ. We ask this through Christ our Lord. Amen.

St. Charles Borromeo; St. Aloysius

CHARLES BORROMEO was born in a castle in Arona, Italy in 1538. He studied at an abbey and received a doctorate in canon law in 1552. His uncle, Pope Pius IV, made him the cardinal and archbishop of Milan at age twenty-two. He was ordained and made a bishop in 1563. He established schools, hospitals, seminaries, a community of oblates for the sanctity of priests and a religious education program for youth. As bishop, he held over ten synods, organized relief efforts to alleviate famine and plague and personally fed 3,000 famine victims daily for three months. A major figure in the Counter Reformation, he implemented the teachings of the Council of Trent on doctrine and the liturgy and participated in writing the Roman Catechism. His catechetical teachings and pastoral visitations brought many Catholics back to the Church. He died in 1584 and was canonized in 1610. St. Aloysius Gonzaga, born in 1568 in Lombardy, Italy received his First Holy Communion from St. Charles. A royal page, he aspired to the religious life and joined the Jesuits in 1585. He was a model of purity known for his heroic charity and penance. He died from a plague in 1591 while caring for plague victims in Rome. He was canonized in 1726 and is the patron of Catholic youth.

St. Charles Borromeo

O Lord, may the pastoral zeal of Thy Confessor and Bishop, St. Charles, set before the Church the example of a faithful shepherd whose love for the Church and wealth of teaching guides the flock of Christ to the glory of eternal life. Amen.

St. Aloysius Gonzaga

O God, grant that, through the merits and prayers of St. Aloysius, we may follow his angelic life of innocence and his spirit of penance and come to the heavenly banquet to dwell in Thy courts forever. Amen.

The Child Jesus

THE CHILD JESUS, Who was born of the House of David, is both God and Man, the Son of the eternal Father, and the Son of the Virgin Mary. He assumed human nature to become the Lamb of God to take away the sins of the world and to be the author of the generation and restoration of divine life in souls. He teaches us to become a child of God the Father, to live for God, to obey His divine law and to preserve the grace of innocence in renouncing the deceptions of the world, the flesh and the devil. In His Heart are found all the treasures of wisdom and understanding. The Child Jesus was seen in the miracle of the sun at Fátima on Oct. 13, 1917. He and His Mother on Dec. 10, 1925 told Sr. Lucy, the surviving seer of the Fátima visions, to console the Heart of Mary through the devotion of five consecutive First Saturdays. On Feb. 15, 1926, the Child Jesus said He was pleased with those who make reparation to the Immaculate Heart of Mary. Through His incarnation and birth, the Child Jesus, God the Son made man, is the light of God's salvation shining upon all mankind.

Prayer to the Child Jesus

O most holy Child Jesus, I know You love me and come near me to make me a child of God. You are my teacher and savior who never leaves me and always gives me hope. I believe You are the Prince of Peace and I learn from You to treasure the sacred gift of childhood as a sign of my eternal destiny in heaven in union with Your Father. Lord Jesus, may I love You more. Amen.

The Divine Child

A Child is born to us, a Son is given to us and upon His shoulders kingship rests. The Lord has made known His salvation through the Divine Child of the Virgin Mary's womb that reveals His justice in the sight of the nations. Our God and Savior, Jesus Christ, became a Child that He might cleanse for Himself an acceptable people. Amen.

Christ the King

CHRIST THE KING is a feast day solemnly instituted in 1925 by Pope Pius XI to proclaim the complete dominion and social reign of Jesus Christ over individuals, families, nations and the world. Christ is the "King and center of all hearts," arrayed in the splendor of the Father, Who subjects the conscience, mind and will of man to divine law to counteract secularism that organizes society as if God did not exist. As the sovereign Lord of creation and Eternal Priest Who overcomes the slavery of sin and death, His royalty is universal. His rule is observed by Christian kings and rulers who uphold the supernatural rights of God and the Church in society. He is the "lion of the tribe of Judah, the Root of David," Who establishes an eternal kingdom, that is not of this world, through the Blood of His cross, His royal scepter of power. Born to "rule over the house of Jacob," Christ sacrifices Himself to give testimony to the truth of the kingdom of God and win the crown of everlasting life. He will come again to judge the world as King of kings and Lord of lords, the great King above all gods. Through Him, the faithful win a glorious victory over the powers of hell and, in the regal splendor of His heavenly court, worship before the throne of His Sacred Heart.

Christ the King

Almighty and eternal God, Who through Thy beloved Son, the sovereign King of the whole world, has willed to restore all things in Him, mercifully grant that all the nations that are divided by sin may be brought to unity under the dominion of His loving rule. Who lives and reigns with the Father and the Holy Spirit, for ever and ever. Amen.

The Lamb Once Slain

The Lamb that was slain is worthy to receive power and divinity and wisdom and strength and honor; to Him be glory and riches for ever and ever. Give to the King, O God, Thy justice and to the King's Son Thy judgment. Amen.

Et Ipse est ante omnia

St. Clare of Assisi

CLARE was born in 1194 in Assisi, Italy. She was the daughter of a noble, and at age eighteen was inspired by a sermon of St. Francis to leave all things for Christ and embrace holy poverty. She accepted a penitential habit from St. Francis, and despite family opposition, remained resolute in her vocation. In 1215, Clare moved to a house near the San Damiano church and founded the order of the Poor Clares, where her widowed mother and two of her sisters joined the community. Members of her order were to mortify themselves by walking barefoot, sleeping on the ground and always abstaining from meat. Clare was visited by many bishops and popes during the forty years she was abbess, and she firmly insisted on the absolute renunciation of property in her rule of life. During an attempted siege of her convent, she repelled an invading army by holding the Blessed Sacrament at the convent gate. Clare was a translucent example of Franciscan spirituality in her love for holy poverty and in the contemplation of Christ, Who "will keep your virginity ever unspotted." She died in 1253 and was canonized in 1255. Clare believed that "he who loves temporal things loses the fruit of love." The observance of the penitential practices of the Poor Clares have made them powerful intercessors before God.

St. Clare, Virgin

God our Father, You chose the consecrated soul of St. Clare as a victim of expiation and praise in Your Son's great work of Redemption. May we follow her in the spirit of holy poverty and come to the vision of Your eternal glory. Through Christ our Lord. Amen.

Prayer to St. Clare

Dear St. Clare, wise and prudent virgin, help us to make good use of our time to know and do the holy will of God, that we may refrain from the excessive use of television and live morally upright lives in the service of God's truth. We ask this through Christ our Lord. Amen.

David and Goliath

DAVID, the youngest of the eight sons of Jesse of Bethlehem, was a charming, young shepherd whom the prophet Samuel anointed to be the future King of Israel. He was an excellent harpist and speaker and the spirit of the Lord was upon him. In a battle between the Israelites and the Philistines, a giant named Goliath challenged the Israelites to send one man into battle with him to determine which side would be the victor. While on an errand to bring food to three of his brothers in the battle, David heard Goliath's challenge and his insults against the armies of the Lord. With his faith in the living God, David volunteered to avenge the insults and to fight the giant the way he slew wild animals. He set aside the armor that was too hard to wear and went into battle with a staff, a sling and five round stones from the wadi in his shepherd's bag. He declared, in the name of the Lord, that he would strike Goliath down. David flung a single stone with his sling that struck Goliath dead in the forehead and then cut off the giant's head. God was glorified through David's staff and sling which prefigures Christ's cross that defeats the "prince of this world," and Mary's Rosary that can crush the head of Satan with a single Hail Mary.

The Lord is God

Lord, You have been our refuge from generation unto generation. Before the mountains were made or the earth and the world was formed, You are God from eternity to eternity. I have hoped in Your word to execute judgment on the wicked. Help me, O Lord, my God. Amen. Alleluia.

Bless the Lord

Bless the Lord, O my soul, and never forget all His benefits. May my youth be renewed like that of an eagle. Let my heart rejoice to seek the Lord and be strengthened to seek His face evermore. Give glory to the Lord and call upon His Name that His justice be proclaimed. Amen.

Jesus, Mary, Joseph assist me in my last agony!

The Death of Joseph

ST. JOSEPH, the spouse of the Virgin Mary and the foster father of Jesus, God the Son made man, is the last of the patriarchs to lead, guide and protect the covenant of God that is fulfilled in Jesus. Joseph was not the New Adam, but at the message of an angel, he became the guardian of the mystery of the incarnation of Life itself. He anticipated the sufferings of Jesus in the prophecy of Simeon and, like Moses, delivered the family of God out of its exile in Egypt to the promised land and was privileged to behold the face of God. He was the father of the hidden life of Jesus until His public ministry began when the Father proclaimed Him "My Son." Joseph was a just man favored by God who lived and died in the presence of God and the Mother of God. He surrendered himself at death into the hands of Jesus and Mary in gratitude and in joy to God Who entrusted him with the care of His Son. After death, he entered the abode of the just and confidently awaited deliverance into the promised land of heaven that came through the resurrection of Jesus. Joseph is the patron of a happy death and of the Universal Church who safely leads the children of God through the valley of darkness to the eternal home of heaven.

Prayer for a Happy Death

O my Lord and Savior, support me in my last hour by the strong arms of Thy sacraments and the fragrance of Thy consolations. Let Thy absolving words be said over me and the holy oil sign and seal me. Let Thine own Body be my food and Thy Blood my sprinkling and let Thy Mother Mary come to me and my angel whisper peace to me and Thy glorious saints and my own dear patrons smile on me, that in and through them all I may die as I desire to live, in Thy Church, in Thy faith and in Thy love. Amen.

St. Dominic

ST. DOMINIC was born in Calaruega, Spain in 1170. He was the son of a knight, and his greatness was foretold in the vision of a running dog lighting up the world with a torch and by a star seen above his forehead at baptism. At age seven, Dominic was schooled in the classics in a town that was on the road that led to the shrine of St. James at Compostela. He devoted himself to prayer and study during his university years, and sold some of his books to help feed the poor. At twenty-five, he entered the religious life and was ordained in 1195. He travelled with a bishop in 1203 to preach against the Albigensian heresy, and later founded an order of preachers which combined penance, prayer and study for the purpose of saving souls through the preaching and teaching of God's word. According to tradition, the Blessed Virgin told him to preach the devotion of the Holy Rosary, "the psalter of the lay people," as an effective weapon against heresy. His order included friars and nuns, and was approved by Pope Honorius III. Many converted to the Catholic faith through his preaching and his miraculous power. He once blessed a well which restored health to the sick that drank from it. He died in 1221 and was canonized in 1234. In the first hundred years of the Dominican order, 13,000 members were martyred.

St. Dominic, Confessor

O God, through the merits and teaching of St. Dominic, Your devoted Confessor, Your Church was gloriously acclaimed. Grant that, through his intercession, she may always advance in her spiritual and temporal mission of salvation. Through Christ our Lord. Amen.

Prayer to St. Dominic

O most holy priest of God, St. Dominic, you are the beloved son of the Queen of heaven who worked many miracles. Intercede for my needs before the Mother of the most Holy Rosary and her eternal Son that I may obtain the favor I ask. Amen.

The Four Evangelists

THE EVANGELISTS MATTHEW, MARK, LUKE AND JOHN, symbolized by a man, a lion, an ox and an eagle, are the four inspired Gospel writers that proclaim the "Good News" of Jesus Christ. Matthew traces the origin of Jesus from Abraham to Joseph and says that the kingdom of heaven begins with Jesus and is definitively fulfilled in His Second Coming at the end of time. The community of believers in Jesus forms the Church which is built on the Apostle Peter. Mark wrote his Gospel from the teachings of St. Peter in which Jesus, the Son of God, is enthroned as King of the world on Calvary and is vindicated in His resurrection. Luke shows the compassion and mercy of Jesus and that salvation is possible for anyone who believes in Jesus. Man's union with God begins with the incarnation of Jesus and is continued through grace and prayer. John declares that Jesus is the eternal Word made flesh, the Lamb of God, Who is the "I am" of salvation that reveals the Father. He is the temple of God and the revelation of Truth that grants eternal life through the gift of the Holy Spirit. The Church has the mission to teach about the commands, miracles and parables of Jesus and to preach His Gospel to the ends of the earth.

The Four Gospels

O God, may the inspired writing of the Gospels increase love for Thy Word and fidelity to Thy commands through the teaching authority of the Church that her mission of preaching the divine revelation of Jesus will reveal His life in the world. Through Christ Jesus, Who is Lord for ever and ever. Amen.

The Light of Salvation

The heavens declare Thy wonders, O Lord. May Thy Name be great among the nations that all people will praise Thee. May Thy salvation be known upon the earth for there is no one beside Thee. Thy truth endures forever and Thy light shines upon the earth through Thy servants. Praise the God of our salvation.

The Message of Fátima

SISTER LUCY DOS SANTOS, born in 1907, is the living witness of the six apparitions approved by the Church of Our Lady of the Rosary at Fátima, Portugal from May to October 1917. She was one of three children to whom Our Lady appeared and delivered an apocalyptic message of the annihilation of nations that could be prevented through a daily Rosary, penance and the consecration of Russia to her Immaculate Heart. Our Lady said God wished to establish in the world devotion to her Immaculate Heart to lead souls to heaven, to convert sinners, to make Communions of reparation on the First Saturdays of the month and to bring about a period of peace in the world and the conversion of Russia. Her message was confirmed on Oct. 13 by the many conversions that resulted from a miracle in which the sun fell from its orbit but resumed its normal course before engulfing the earth in fire. Through the Heart of Mary, God transmits the grace of salvation and in her Heart dwells Jesus, the peace and salvation of the world. Her Heart is a refuge for souls and the prophesied triumph of her Immaculate Heart will be a supernatural assent to the truths of the Catholic faith.

Consecration to the Immaculate Heart of Mary

O Immaculate Heart of Mary, refuge of sinners and comfort of the afflicted, I consecrate myself to thee and offer thee a daily Rosary along with my sacrifices for the conversion of sinners. I promise to be faithful to my baptismal promises, to renounce the devil and to receive Holy Communion on the First Saturdays of the month in reparation for the sins committed against thee and thy Son. May thy Immaculate Heart reign over me and make my heart like thine where the Heart of thy Son reigned and triumphed. In thy Heart, O Mary, full of grace, dwells the triumph of the kingdom of God in the world. May my consecration to thy Immaculate Heart hasten the day of peace on earth that all people will bless thee and praise the glorious victory of the Heart of Jesus. Amen.

Blessed Faustina Kowalska

BLESSED SISTER MARY FAUSTINA KOWALSKA was born on Aug. 25, 1905 in the small village of Glogowiec, Poland. Her baptismal name was Helen, and at the age of seven she heard God calling her to the religious life. At eighteen, she asked her parents for permission to enter a convent, but they refused. She remained in the world, trying to understand God's call. Then she heard a voice calling her to Warsaw, where, on Aug. 1, 1925, she became a postulant in the Congregation of the Sisters of Our Lady of Mercy and made her perpetual vows on May 1, 1933. During her convent life, she did baking, gardening and was a gatekeeper, and experienced much physical and spiritual suffering. She received many spiritual communications from Jesus Who asked her to spread devotion to The Divine Mercy, especially through a chaplet and a painting. She died in Cracow on Oct. 5, 1938 and was beatified on Mercy Sunday, Apr. 18, 1993 by Pope John Paul II who began the Informative Process for her cause while he was Archbishop of Cracow.

Prayer for Mercy

O Jesus, font of Mercy, ever flowing from Your Sacred Heart, Your Divine Heart is Mercy itself. May I know the depth of Your merciful love, which has redeemed the world. Your mercy is my sanctity and salvation that gives You great glory. You, O Divine Jesus, are the delight and joy of my whole being. Have mercy on me, for I have sinned in Your sight. With the help of Your grace and the prayers of Blessed Sr. Faustina, I will worship Your Divine Mercy, and patiently submit to Your divine will, which is nourishment for my soul. Glory, praise and honor to The Divine Mercy of Jesus, now and forever. Amen.

St. Francis de Sales; St. Jane

ST. FRANCIS DE SALES was born near Annecy, France in 1567. He earned a doctorate in civil law, but abandoned a secular career to become a priest in 1593. He began a five year mission to the Calvinists that won him thousands of converts. In 1599, he was made co-adjutor bishop of Geneva and succeeded to the see in 1602. He established a seminary and instructed his priests to preach and teach the faith in simple language. A man of great meekness and modesty, Francis taught that holiness is possible in any state of life and he published many ascetical writings, among them his spiritual classics *The Introduction to the Devout Life* and *The Treatise on Divine Love*. He died in 1622, was canonized in 1665 and declared a Doctor of the Church in 1877. St. Jane Frances de Chantal was born in Dijon, France in 1572. She was married in 1592, raised seven children and was happily married for eight years. After her husband died, she met St. Francis de Sales, a spiritual friend, and after making suitable provisions for her children, followed his direction in founding the order of the Visitation. Sixty convents were established during her lifetime. She died in 1641 and was canonized in 1767.

St. Francis de Sales

O God, by Thy will, St. Francis de Sales, Confessor and Bishop, was all things to all men for the salvation of souls, grant that, being filled with Thy love, we may follow his counsels and benefit from the merits of his gentle wisdom to inherit the grace of everlasting life. Through Christ our Lord. Amen.

St. Jane de Chantal

Enkindle in us, O Lord, that divine fire of the Holy Spirit which consumed the soul of Francis de Sales and enlightened the heart of St. Jane Frances de Chantal that the grace of Thy incarnation may be welcomed in the hearts of all mankind. We ask this through Christ our Lord. Amen.

Blessed Gianna Beretta Molla

BLESSED GIANNA BERETTA MOLLA, a pediatrician from Milan and mother of three children, at the age of thirty-nine, decided to carry her fourth child to term rather than undergo the removal of a tumor that would have required the abortion of her child. Seven days after she gave birth to a girl named Gianna Emanuela, who is still living today, Gianna Molla died on Apr. 28, 1962. She sacrificed her life to give birth to her unborn child and acted as a mother, doing everything to save her child. In union with the sacrifice of Jesus, her love for life was faithful unto death. She accepted the child as a gift of God and would not let inconvenience abort her child's right to life. In light of her generosity, her life-giving charity transcends the social forces of vanity and brings forth a ray of light into a prevailing culture of death. In Gianna, gratitude is given to God for the gift of the child and life is given that another may live. She is a heroic model of fidelity to the dignity and vocation of a woman as wife and mother. She was beatified by Pope John Paul II in May 1993.

Prayer for Childbirth

Heavenly Father, Creator of human life, may the example and prayers of Blessed Gianna, who sacrificed her life to give life to her innocent unborn child and who chose to bring her child to term out of her love for Your gift of the child as well as the child's right to be born and baptized into Your kingdom, inspire mothers with difficult pregnancies to have the courage to bring their children to term and after birth to give them the love they deserve. Through Christ our Lord. Amen.

The Good Shepherd

THE GOOD SHEPHERD is Jesus, the only Son of God Who became man, and laid down His life to gather the sheep straying in the bondage of sin into the one sheepfold of His Church founded on the rock of the Apostle Peter. Jesus knows and loves His sheep and they know and love Him. He feeds them with the gift and grace of His eternal life, His own Sacred Body and Most Precious Blood in the Holy Eucharist. He guides His flock through the teaching authority of His Church, where the sheep hear and follow His voice, the voice of the Shepherd and guardian of their souls, because "I know mine and mine know Me." He is the Shepherd Who laid down His life to redeem one flock, and apart from His rule the sheep can not be saved. He enfolds His sheep in the arms of His gentle, loving care, and they trust that His staff will protect them from evil. The Good Shepherd leads His sheep through the valleys and hills of life to His eternal pasture, where they will wear white robes washed in "the blood of the Lamb." The Good Shepherd is the Lamb of salvation Who leads His flock to the springs of everlasting life flowing from His Most Sacred Heart.

The Good Shepherd

The Lord is my Shepherd; there is nothing I shall want. He gives me rest in fresh green pastures. He leads me near restful waters to restore my drooping spirit. He guides me along right paths; He is true to His word. If I should walk in the shadow of darkness, no evil shall I fear. You are there with the strength of Your staff, which gives me Your comfort. You have served me a banquet in the presence of my foes. You have anointed my head with oil; my cup overflows. Surely goodness and kindness will follow me everyday of my life. In the Lord's own temple I will dwell, for ever and ever.

St. Hermenegild

ST. HERMENEGILD was born the son of Leovigild, an Arian King of Spain. His father made him a prince of his Visigothic kingdom in Seville, and he married a devout Catholic, the daughter of the King of Austrasia in France. Through her example and the teaching of St. Leander, Archbishop of Seville, he was converted from his Arianism to the Catholic faith. His father, upon hearing of his son's new found faith, decided to take away his duties and possessions, and even his life if he refused to return to Arian beliefs. But he refused, and his father had him put in prison, charging him with the offense of heresy. During Eastertime in 586, he sent an Arian bishop to his son, hoping to win his favor if he would receive Holy Communion from the bishop. Hermenegild declined, and his father, in a burst of anger, had the young prince put to death. St. Hermenegild died a martyr of the Holy Eucharist rather than renounce his Catholic faith in the consubstantiality of the Word of God. St. Gregory the Great credits him with the conversion of Visigothic Spain and his brother, Reccared, a son of Leovigild. His feast day is Apr. 13.

St. Hermenegild, Martyr

O God, Who inspired blessed Hermenegild, Thy martyr, to choose the Kingdom of Heaven rather than an earthy throne, grant us, we beseech Thee, that, following his example, we may despise the fleeting things of the world and of time and follow after those that are eternal. We ask this through our Lord Jesus Christ, Thy Son, Who lives and reigns with Thee in the unity of the Holy Spirit, one God, for ever and ever. Amen.

"I am the Resurrection"

"I AM THE RESURRECTION AND THE LIFE," Jesus says. He is the Lord of Life, the fullness of life and existence itself, Who rose from the dead on the third day *"sicut dixit,"* and to Whom is due the homage of "my Lord and my God." The resurrection of Jesus Christ from the dead is not a return to a previously lived life or a miraculous resuscitation. It is the beginning of a new life for man in which the Risen Christ enters His glory at the right hand of the Father. The resurrection is a doctrine of faith necessary for salvation and without which the Church's faith is meaningless. In His resurrection from the dead, the Crucified and Risen Christ appears to His disciples who touch, speak and eat with Him. His resurrection anticipates the resurrection of the dead at the end of the world, when those who are worthy of Christ and His love will rise to an eternal communion of love and life in Him. They will be reconstituted in a glorified body not subject to the limitations of an earthly or cosmic existence. They will be under the rule of the Holy Spirit Who glorifies the victory of "the Lamb once slain." The resurrection of Jesus Christ from the dead frees mankind from the slavery of sin and death and promises the grace of eternal life to those who live for Him.

The Glory of the Lord

O God, Who illumines the world by the glory of the Lord's Resurrection, preserve in the new children of Thy family the spirit of adoption which Thou hast given, that renewed in body and mind, they may render to Thee a pure and fitting service. Through Jesus Christ our Lord Who lives for ever and ever. Amen.

The Eternal Gate

O God, Who through Thine only-begotten Son, has conquered sin and death and opened the gates of everlasting life, grant that Thy servants may always adhere to the glorious mystery of the Lord's Resurrection which they have received by faith. We ask this through Christ our Lord. Amen.

Blessed Imelda

IMELDA was born to a wealthy family in Bologna, Italy in 1322. On her fifth birthday, she told her parents of her desire to receive Holy Communion even though fourteen was the required age. She committed herself to the study of the Catholic faith and decided to become a Dominican nun. At the age of nine, she was admitted to a Dominican convent and frequently prayed for Jesus to come and dwell in her soul. One day in 1333, while kneeling in the convent chapel, a consecrated Host appeared in a splendid light over the altar and going forth came to rest above Imelda's head, where she gazed upon It in ecstasy. She remained kneeling for a long time, desiring to receive Jesus in Holy Communion. A priest was summoned to give Imelda the Host. She received the Host and continued to kneel for a very long time, prompting the Mother Superior to determine the reason why. She found that Imelda had died. Out of her great love for Jesus, she died after receiving her First Holy Communion. Imelda was beatified by Pope Leo XII in 1826 and is the patroness of First Holy Communicants.

After Holy Communion

Jesus, You are my Lord and my God. I thank You for coming to visit me in the real presence of Your Body, Blood, Soul and Divinity. I ask, through the prayers of Blessed Imelda, that You will reign over my heart and never let me be separated from You. May I serve You faithfully that I may adore and glorify You forever in heaven. Amen.

Prayer of Thanksgiving

Dear Jesus, I thank Thee for nourishing me with Thy Sacred Body and Most Precious Blood. I am grateful for the blessings I have received through the merits of Thy Passion applied to my soul in the Holy Sacrifice of the Mass. May my devotion to Thee in this sacrament of Thy love make me adhere to Thy will and become more like Thee. Amen.

St. Jerome

JEROME was born in 342 in the small Dalmatian town of Stridon. His father taught him the ways of piety, and then sent him to Rome for study, where he mastered the classical languages of Latin and Greek, and became an orator. He was baptized, and then travelled with friends to further his studies. He spent four years in a Syrian desert in prayer and study with the virtuous Abbot Theodosius, and learned to overcome temptations of the flesh. While in Antioch in 377, he was ordained a priest. He studied the scriptures under St. Gregory Nazianzen in Constantinople, and then attended a council in Rome called by Pope St. Damascus, who later made him his secretary. Jerome wrote a book defending the perpetual virginity of Mary. In 385, he set sail for the Holy Land, and lived in a cave-like cell near the birthplace of Jesus, studying Sacred Scripture and directing a monastery in Bethlehem founded by St. Paula. St. Jerome is a Father and Doctor of the Church, renowned for his translation of Sacred Scripture into Latin, the *Vulgate* version approved by Pope St. Gregory the Great. He died in Bethlehem on Sept. 30, 420, and is the patron of librarians.

St. Jerome, Doctor of the Church

O God, Who in holy and blessed Jerome, Thy Confessor, did provide for Thy Church a great and venerable teacher for expounding the truth of Sacred Scripture, grant we beseech Thee, that through his merits and prayers we may be able, by the help of Thy grace, to practice what he taught by word and example. Through Christ our Lord. Amen.

Jesus is Laid in the Tomb

AFTER Jesus was taken down from the Cross and placed in the arms of His Mother, Joseph of Arimathea and Nicodemus brought the linen and spices for the burial of Jesus. They wrapped His body in the linen along with the spices and carried Him to Joseph's new tomb that was hewn out in a rock. Mary, the Mother of Jesus, Mary Magdalen and some of the holy women of Jerusalem accompanied them. According to tradition, the apostle John was joined in the procession to the tomb by the apostles Peter and James, and along the way, all creation mourned the death of Him through Whom all things were made. The trees and flowers bent in homage, the birds sang a melancholy song, the ground trembled, the sun dimmed its light and the angels bowed in adoration. The Passion of Jesus began and ended in a garden. He was the seed of eternal life placed in a sepulcher from which death would die through His resurrection from the dead. Our hearts must be the new resting place for the Risen Body of Christ in Holy Communion, an abode uncontaminated by the world that we must guard with the immutable truth of Christ and the fragrant grace of Christian virtue.

The Passion of Jesus

O God, Who left us a record of Thy Passion in the holy shroud, wherein Joseph wrapped Thy Sacred Body when taken down from the Cross, mercifully grant that through Thy death and burial we may be brought to the glory of Thy resurrection. Through Christ our Lord. Amen.

The Good Sower

O God, Who by the voice of the holy Prophets has declared to all the children of Thy Church that Thou art the Sower of good seed and the Cultivator of chosen branches, grant to Thy people who are Thy vine and harvestfield, that they may root out all thorns and briars and produce good fruit in abundance. We ask this through Christ our Lord. Amen.

St. Joan of Arc

JOAN OF ARC, *Jeanne-la-Puelle*, a consecrated daughter of God, was born in Domrémy, France on Jan. 6, 1412. She was a shepherd girl, the youngest of five children of Jacques D'arc. Joan was a chaste, reverent, gentle, yet courageous Christian who, at a young age, heard the heavenly Voices of saints calling her to receive the sacraments frequently and to undertake the liberation of France from the occupation of the British. Convinced of her heavenly mission, she sought permission from the exiled King of France to begin her military campaign. He agreed, and she rode into battle dressed in white armor, riding a horse and bearing a banner that read "Jesus, Mary" and "In the Name of the King of Heaven." Her army won impressive victories, most notably at Orleans, which resulted in the restoration of the King who was crowned at Rheims on July 17, 1429. Joan lost a battle in Paris and then was captured by the British. She was tried by a Church court where many testified against the credibility of her mission and her Catholic faith. She was falsely condemned as a heretic and delivered to the civil authorities who had her burned with fire on May 30, 1431. The Church re-opened her case in 1456 and found her innocent. She was canonized in 1920 and is a patroness of France.

St. Joan of Arc, Virgin

Lord our God, You have blessed us with the heroic life of Joan, Your holy Virgin, to defend the Catholic faith and her country from the snares of her enemies. Grant that, through her intercession, Your Church may enjoy the peace and unity it signifies. We ask this through Christ our Lord. Amen.

St. John the Baptist

JOHN THE BAPTIST, the forerunner and precursor of Jesus Christ, was the son of Zachary, a Jewish priest, and Elizabeth, a cousin of the Virgin Mary, and was born in Ain-Karim six months before Jesus. As an unborn child, "filled with the Holy Spirit from his mother's womb," John leapt for joy upon seeing Jesus in the womb of Mary when she came to visit Elizabeth. At that moment, he was pre-sanctified, and was born without Original Sin, a birthday celebrated in the Church since the 4th century. His name and birth was revealed by the angel Gabriel, and in thanksgiving his father uttered the *Benedictus*. John was consecrated to the Lord from birth. He lived in solitude in a desert in Judea, where he wore penitential garments, and at age twenty-seven began preaching a baptism of repentance at the Jordan river. He spoke in the spirit and power of Elijah, "for the kingdom of God is at hand." When he baptized Jesus, heralding Him as "the Lamb of God Who takes away the sin of the world," the heavens opened, a dove descended and the Father said "this is My Son." Jesus declared that there is "no greater prophet born of woman" than John. He was martyred by King Herod, and was the last of the great prophets, a fearless teacher and a virgin, who was commissioned to inaugurate the coming of God's kingdom.

St. John the Baptist, Martyr

May Thy holy Church, O Lord, rejoice at the birth of John the Baptist who prepared the way for Jesus, the Author of salvation, and through his prayers, may she always courageously teach that the unborn child is the fruit of true love. We ask this through Christ our Lord. Amen.

The Herald of God

O St. John the Baptist, undefiled herald proclaiming the reign of God's kingdom, help us to be faithful to our promises of baptism in rejecting the world, the flesh and the devil, that we may follow the teaching of Jesus that leads to eternal life. This we ask through Christ our Lord. Amen.

St. John Neumann

JOHN NEPOMUCENE NEUMANN, the "sturdy mountain boy," was born Mar. 28, 1811 in Prachatiz, Bohemia. He was drawn to the religious life and entered a seminary in Prague, but could not be ordained due to an overabundance of priests in Bohemia. In 1836, he came to the Unites States and was ordained in New York. He spent much time in mission work among German Catholics. He joined the Redemptorists in 1840 and became the American superior in 1847. He was named the fourth bishop of Philadelphia in 1852 and built many churches, schools, established a seminary and founded an order of sisters of St. Francis. He was the first to publish the *Kyriale* in the United States and wrote two catechisms approved by the American bishops that were extensively used in Catholic schools. In his diocese, vespers was sung in the churches on Sunday, the clergy attended an annual retreat, and in 1853 Forty Hours devotion began among the parishes. Bishop Neumann believed in personally bringing Christ to his flock through frequent pastoral visits. He died in 1860 and was canonized June 19, 1977. His motto was "Passion of Christ, strengthen me."

Bishop St. John Neumann

God our Father, may the goodness, generosity, charity and sacrifice exemplified in the life of Bishop Neumann encourage all bishops to a life of dedication, zeal and fidelity to Thy Son, Jesus Christ, and His Church. We ask this through Jesus Christ our Lord. Amen.

Prayer for Holiness

Lord Jesus Christ, may the worship of Thy divine mysteries lead the faithful to a greater holiness of life and a deeper understanding of Thy teachings for which St. John Neumann labored to bring honor and glory to Thy Name. Amen.

Blessed Juan Diego

JUAN DIEGO, born in 1474 near Mexico City with the name Cuauhtlatohuac meaning "the eagle who speaks," was baptized in 1525 along with his wife and uncle. On his way to morning Mass on Dec. 9, 1531, the Spanish feast of the Immaculate Conception, Juan heard music from Tepeyac hill and saw a beautiful lady standing before a bright white cloud who said, "I am truly the perpetual and perfect Virgin Mary, holy mother of the true God through whom everything lives." She told Juan to ask the bishop to build a church on the hill. The bishop said that he needed a sign, and on Dec. 12 Our Lady told Juan to gather the flowers blooming on the hillside into his tilma, and after she arranged them, to show them to the bishop. When Juan opened his tilma, the bishop saw red roses fall to the floor and beheld a miraculous portrait of Our Lady on the tilma. He gave permission to build a chapel and Juan became the guardian of the heavenly treasure and the evangelizer of millions of Aztecs who were converted to the Catholic faith. The holy image, known as Our Lady of Guadalupe, was a sign that she who crushes the stone serpent and overcomes the mother-goddess with the purity of her faith, will gather into the mantle of her heavenly protection the fragrant flowers of faith in her Son. Juan died in 1548 and was beatified May 6, 1990.

Mother of the True God

Most Holy Mary, ever Virgin and Mother of the living and true God Who became man for our salvation, may the Church, built on the faith of Peter, become a flower garden of sanctity through the prayers of Blessed Juan Diego, your spiritual son, where new flowers of divine faith will be planted to glorify Your Son and honor you as the mother of mankind. Amen.

King David

DAVID, the youngest son of Jesse, was born in Bethlehem around 1040 B.C. He was a shepherd who killed a bear and a lion to protect his father's flock. As a youth, he was anointed by the prophet Samuel to be the future King of Israel. An occasional harpist and servant for King Saul, David became famous when he stood alone to defend the fortunes of Israel and killed a Philistine giant named Goliath. David entered the king's service and became a warrior and his power and fame grew as he won impressive military battles. King Saul became envious and sought to destroy David. But David escaped and after Saul was killed in a battle, he established his throne in Hebron and then in Jerusalem as the King of Israel. He built a tabernacle for the Ark of the Covenant and made plans to build a temple for the worship of God. Although David ruled with great equity and justice, favored by God as "a man after my own heart," he was chastised by the prophet Nathan for committing adultery and repented. David reigned as king for forty years and died in 970 B.C. He was the "sweet psalmist of Israel," and the ancestor of Jesus Christ, the root of Jesse, Who was born of the House of David in Bethlehem and Whose kingdom has no end.

The Reign of God

O God, You have made known Your salvation in the sight of the nations. Your anointed One, Jesus, born of the House of David, rules forever in the kingdom of God. He comes to reconcile all things in Himself, making peace through the Blood of His Cross. He alone is the alpha and omega of all that is. Praise to Jesus Christ, our King. Amen.

The Coming of the King

Lift up your gates, O princes. O eternal gates, let the King of glory enter. Thy throne, O God, is everlasting, for behold Thy King comes, the Savior of the world. In Him, we have remission of our sins and are made worthy partakers of His eternal love and life. He shall reign as King for ever and shall bless His people with peace. Amen.

St. Lawrence

LAWRENCE was born in Spain and became one of the seven deacons to serve Pope St. Sixtus II in Rome. He was entrusted with the care of the poor and the Church treasury. In the year 258 before his martyrdom, Pope Sixtus told Lawrence to sell the Church property and give the money to the poor. A Roman official heard of the exchange and insisted that Church property belonged to the Emperor. Lawrence presented to the official his beneficiaries, the poor people, who he said were the Church's wealth. The official was upset with Lawrence's embarrassing display of wealth and had Lawrence scourged, racked and fastened to a gridiron, where he was slowly roasted to death. During his suffering, Lawrence prayed for his persecutors and told them to turn him over, since he was sufficiently roasted on one side. Lawrence died a martyr for the sake of the poor. He is commemorated in the Canon of the Mass and is one of the most celebrated saints in the Church.

St. Lawrence, Martyr

O almighty God, we implore Thee to mercifully extinguish the flames of our vices even as You gave Your servant Lawrence the grace to overcome the fires of his torments and merit eternal salvation. We ask this through Christ our Lord. Amen.

Prayer to St. Lawrence

O glorious St. Lawrence, cheerful giver in the service of the poor, by your prayers, may we be purified by the cross of Christ that we may die to ourselves to bear the fruits of true justice. This we ask through our Lord Jesus Christ. Amen.

God's Deliverance

From the oppression of the flames of sin, I was not burnt.

The Little Flower

THÉRÈSE OF THE CHILD JESUS AND THE HOLY FACE was canonized a saint on May 17, 1925 in St. Peter's Basilica by Pope Pius XI who also beatified her two years earlier. During the ceremony, roses that decorated the lights in the apse fell to the floor in an unknown way which was a sign that Thérèse was keeping her promise that "after my death I will let fall a shower of roses." Her roses were the little favors she granted to souls through her intercession, especially for missionaries and for the welfare of the Church. Thérèse began her consecrated life to God when she entered the Carmelite convent at Lisieux in 1888 to save souls and to pray for priests. She offered herself as a victim to God's merciful love so that souls would love God for all eternity. She believed in the "little way" of spiritual childhood, of humility and simplicity in all things in order to recognize her nothingness and her dependence on God. Thérèse made the love of God the mainspring of every action and accepted the crosses of life since "in this world there is no fruitfulness without suffering." In the cloistered garden of Carmel, she brought forth the flowers of Christian virtue, and the sweet fragrance of her roses drew others to the love of Jesus in Bethlehem, on Calvary and the Altar.

Prayer to St. Thérèse

Dear St. Thérèse, the Little Flower in God's heavenly garden, obtain from the Heart of Jesus, thy beloved Spouse, the favor I ask (*make your request*). Send me a rose of love that I will become more a child of God and serve the Church through my prayers that you may shower upon the Church roses of grace and virtue that God may be known and loved on earth and glorified forever in heaven. Amen.

St. Louis de Montfort

ST. LOUIS MARIE GRIGNION DE MONTFORT was born in 1673 in Montfort, France. He was educated by the Jesuits and ordained in 1700. He became a chaplain and then organized a group of women later known as the Daughters of Divine Wisdom. St. Louis was gifted with an irresistible prophetic eloquence. His preaching in the street, teaching of catechism and devotion to Mary brought many to his parish missions which consisted of the public recitation of the Rosary, renewal of baptism promises and candlelight processions. He effectively preached on the true devotion to Mary in which one becomes a slave of Jesus through Mary. For a time, he was forbidden to preach in France until Pope Clement XI approved of his missionary apostolate. He became a third order Dominican in 1710 and founded the Company of Mary in 1715. He died in 1716 and was canonized by Pope Pius XII in 1947. His book on *True Devotion to the Blessed Virgin Mary* is a spiritual battle plan for the defeat of the devil through a total consecration to Mary, the divine mould, who forms souls into the likeness of her Son, causing Jesus Christ to triumph.

St. Louis de Montfort

O Most loving Jesus, You have given me Your holy Mother to be my advocate before Your justice. By the prayers of St. Louis de Montfort, may I save my soul in union with Mary who will help me to do Your will and seek Your glory. In her motherly care, may she form Your likeness in my soul unto its fullness. Amen.

Prayer of St. Louis

I am all Thine and all I have is Thine, O most loving Jesus, through Mary, Thy holy Mother. Amen.

The Tree of Life

Happy is the soul in which Mary, the Tree of Life, is planted and which bears her fruit forever. Amen.

Blessed Margaret Castello

BLESSED MARGARET was born in 1287 in Meldola, Italy. She was blind, hunchback and lame and at the age of seven her parents had her imprisoned in a room, isolating her from society because her deformities were an embarrassment to them and dangerous to others. For several years, she was educated by a priest who visited her cell and brought her Holy Communion. She learned to love Jesus and accept her rejection in union with His sufferings. One day, her parents took Margaret to a Franciscan church in the city of Castello, hoping that she would be cured by the day's end. Because her condition remained the same, they abandoned her at the church. Margaret was rescued by families that cared for orphans and was taught how to beg for alms. Her love for God and innocence of life led her to become a third order Dominican. She dedicated her life to prayer and sacrifice, cured the lame and prophesied. During a visit to a prison in Castello, she attended to the prisoners and while praying for them, was raised in ecstasy off the floor to the astonishment of everyone present. Her love for God and neighbor knew no bounds. She died in 1320 and her cult was approved in 1609. She is the patroness of the unwanted, unplanned and unloved.

Blessed Margaret Castello

O God, Your love is everlasting and never leaves us orphans. Through the prayers of Blessed Margaret, may we despise all sin which deforms the soul and cherish the grace and innocence of life that reveals the dignity of the human person created and redeemed by Your Son. We ask this through Christ our Lord. Amen.

Loving His Will

O Lord, before I was, You knew me. You carved me in the palm of Your hand. I am grateful for Your gift of love and life which sustains me and I will meditate on Your commands which I love exceedingly. Your will is my peace and understanding. By Your grace I will glorify Your Name forever. Glory be to God. Amen.

St. Margaret Clitherow

MARGARET CLITHEROW was born at York, England in 1555. She married a wealthy butcher in 1571, raised three children and converted to the Catholic faith. Her husband was fined several times because she refused to support the Church of England and she was held for two years in a prison. Upon her release, Margaret established a Catholic school especially for children and provided a refuge in her home where priests could say Mass and find shelter from the persecutions against Catholics. She was placed under house arrest when she attempted to have her son educated in France. In 1586, she was found guilty of violating the law that prohibited the hiding of Catholic priests, when a search of her home revealed a secret hideout where Mass was said. Because she would not renounce her faith in the priesthood or her devotion to the Holy Sacrifice of the Mass, she was condemned to be crushed to death by an eight hundred pound weight. Margaret Clitherow was among the Forty Martyrs of England and Wales canonized by Pope Paul VI in 1970.

St. Margaret Clitherow

O God, by the love St. Margaret Clitherow had for the Holy Sacrifice of the Mass and the Catholic home, may parents realize their duty as the primary educators of their children to transmit the Catholic faith and make the sacramental life active in their home. We ask this through Christ our Lord. Amen.

Prayer for Priests

Lord Jesus, give Thy priests the grace to work for the sanctification of marriage and family life and the courage to instill in families the faith that teaches them to live for the kingdom of God. Who with the Father and the Holy Spirit lives and reigns in the undivided Trinity forever. Amen.

St. Mark

ST. MARK is one of the four evangelists, who, while in Rome, wrote the Second Gospel in Greek around the year 60 for the gentile converts. His gospel records the life of Jesus Christ according to the teachings of St. Peter, and reveals Jesus as the Divine Son of God. He came from a levitical family and his mother's home was a meeting place for the apostles in Jerusalem. He travelled with Paul and Barnabas, his cousin, on a mission journey to Antioch and Cyprus in the year 44. He met and worked with Sts. Peter and Paul in Rome, and became an interpreter and secretary to St. Peter, who called him "my son Mark." St. Paul said that "he is profitable to me for the ministry." Tradition credits him with establishing the Church in Alexandria, Egypt, where he was martyred in the year 74. He is the patron of Venice and of notaries, and his feast day is Apr. 25. He is symbolized by a lion because his gospel begins with the voice of John the Baptist "crying in the wilderness."

St. Mark, the Evangelist

O God, Who exalted blessed Mark, Thy Evangelist, by the grace of preaching the Gospel, grant, we beseech Thee, that we may ever profit by his teaching and be defended by his prayers. Through Jesus Christ our Lord. Amen.

The Greatest Commandment

Love God with all your heart.

Prayer of Faith

You are the Christ, Lord Jesus, the Son of God. May I not fear to lose my life for Your sake and the Gospel. Like You, may I be a servant to all, and accept little children in Your Name. May I not be ashamed to believe in Your Word that does not pass away, ready to meet You and the angels when You come in the glory of Your Father to judge the world. Amen.

Martha and Mary

MARTHA AND MARY lived in the village of Bethany, east of Jerusalem, where Jesus stayed at their home, was proclaimed "the Son of God" by Martha before raising Lazurus from the dead, and where Jesus was anointed with precious oil and began the journey for His triumphal entry into Jerusalem. On a visit to Martha and Mary, Jesus found Martha busy with "many things" while Mary, her sister, sat at His feet listening to His teaching. Martha asked Jesus to tell Mary to help her with the household tasks. But Jesus said that Mary had "chosen the better part" which shall not be taken from her. Jesus was teaching Martha that feeding the body is not as important as feeding the spiritual needs of the soul, and reminding her that "man does not live on bread alone, but on every word that comes from the mouth of God." Man was made to know, love and serve God and his work must be motivated by prayer which inspires deeds of charity. In the Eucharist, we must open the door of our heart to welcome Jesus into the home of clean heart where He will feed us with His Body and Blood and teach us to be the servants of His love.

Servants of Divine Love

God the Father of our Lord Jesus Christ, give us the grace to believe in the divinely revealed word of Your Son, that nourished by His Body and Blood, we may work and pray for Your glory as the servants of His divine love. We ask this through Christ our Lord. Amen.

Louis and Zélie Martin

LOUIS STANISLAUS MARTIN AND MARIE ZÉLIE GUÉRIN were married in Alençon, France on July 13, 1858. Both had previously desired to enter the religious life but were denied admission. Zélie asked God "to make me a mother of many children and to grant that all of them may be consecrated to Thee." Louis, a watchmaker, and his wife, Zélie, committed themselves to raise children for the glory of God and they dedicated each of their nine children to Mary Immaculate. Four of them died very young, while the others were destined for the convent. Louis called his youngest daughter, Marie Françoise Thérèse, his "little Queen." Louis and Zélie attended daily Mass together, observed the laws of the Church, practiced Christian virtue, prayed in common and cared for the poor. Zélie taught her children how to say their daily prayers. When she died, Louis moved his family to Lisieux. There he would take Thérèse on walks and fishing trips, read and sing to her at home and visit a Carmelite chapel. He encouraged Thérèse in her desire to become a Carmelite nun. At age fifteen, she was admitted to a Carmelite convent where four of her sisters had also entered. Louis gave thanks to God for "the honor He has done me in choosing His spouses from my household." Thérèse was very grateful to her parents for the blessings of a Catholic family life and in the convent she became "the Little Flower" to "offer our Lord the flowers of little sacrifices."

Sanctification of Family Life

O Lord Jesus Christ, Who was subject to Mary and Joseph and sanctified family life with grace and virtue, grant that we may learn from the Holy Family and attain eternal union with Thy family in heaven. Amen.

Peace in the Family

O Lord, through the intercession of Mary, the Mother of God, and blessed Joseph, we ask Thee to establish our families in Thy peace and grace that we may dwell in Thy home and praise Thee for ever and ever. Amen.

Mother Angelica

MOTHER ANGELICA, born Rita Rizzo in Canton, Ohio on Apr. 20, 1923, often suffered from her parents' divorce and from lack of food, adequate shelter and warmth. She graduated from Catholic grade school and helped her mother barely survive in a dry cleaning service. After a miraculous cure of a stomach ailment in 1943, she desired to be a bride of Jesus which led her on Aug. 15, 1944 to enter a Franciscan convent of Perpetual Adoration in Cleveland. She received the name Angelica and made her first profession in Canton in 1947. After recovering from a severe back injury, she fulfilled a promise made to God to build Him a new monastery and raised the funds for it by selling fishing lures. Permission was granted for a new foundation in Birmingham, Alabama where she became abbess of Our Lady of the Angels Monastery in 1962. Known for her perseverance, enthusiasm and blind faith, Mother Angelica entered the communications media to spread God's word and in 1981 founded EWTN, the first nationwide Catholic satellite television station. Through prayer and God's Providence, she has brought the love of Jesus and His truth into the homes of millions in booklets, television, tapes and short-wave radio. In the spirit of St. Francis, she has built up the Church and with childlike faith has been an instrument of God's miraculous grace.

God Alone

To receive You, dear Jesus, in Holy Communion is heaven on earth. I enter into Your Sacred Heart and You become first in my heart. May I attach myself to no one on earth but You alone, Who patiently waits for my undivided love. I belong to You before all others that I will become a child of the Father forever. Amen.

The Love of Jesus

May I love You, Jesus, more each day as I lovingly accept what You will for the good of my soul. I want to walk in Your footsteps and imitate Your love and life. I am confident that Your love is a love that does not fail and I trust in Your love to change the world. Your love, O Jesus, is the life of my soul. Amen.

Mother of Sorrows

OUR LADY, MOTHER OF SORROWS is a feast celebrated on Sept. 15 commemorating the seven sorrows or seven dolors of the Blessed Virgin Mary. The prophecy of Simeon, that her Son was a sign of contradiction destined for the fall and rising of many, was her first sorrow that culminated in the great sorrow of Calvary that pierced her own soul. At the foot of the cross, she was a light shining in the darkness of the human night, that retained belief in her Son's divinity. Like Abraham, she consented to the immolation of her Son, and for the salvation of the world, she suffered with her Son to bring forth God's spiritual children. In union with her sorrowful and Immaculate Heart, we must despise sin, and bear the crosses and trials of life with courage, patience and perseverance. Mary helps us to have true contrition and sorrow for sin, and to ask pardon for offenses committed against God's infinite goodness. The world can not fathom the offering of a Victim to satisfy the justice of God. But Mary, representing us on Calvary, offered prayers of faith and love for the sanctification and salvation of souls that her Son purchased by the shedding of His Precious Blood. She faithfully served the mystery of redemption that flows forth entirely from the merits of her Son, and we remember the indissoluble love of Jesus and Mary suffering for our salvation in the Holy Sacrifice of the Mass.

The Grace of Redemption

O God, at whose passion as Simeon had foretold, a sword of sorrow pierced the sweet soul of Mary, the glorious Virgin Mother, grant that we, who reverently recall her anguish and suffering, may obtain the blessed fruits of Thy redemption. Through Christ our Lord. Amen.

The Heart of Mary

O Most Sorrowful and Immaculate Heart of Mary,
pray for us, now and at the hour of our death. Amen.

Mother Teresa

MOTHER TERESA, Agnes Bojaxhiu, was born on Aug. 27, 1910 in Skopje, Albania. She was raised in a Catholic family and in 1928 joined the Loreto sisters in Ireland. She was sent to teach in India, where she taught for twenty years. On Sept. 10, 1946, she heard God calling her to follow Him in the slums and to serve Him in the poorest of the poor. She was given permission to leave the convent and to lead a religious life among the poor under obedience to the Archbishop of Calcutta. She began a school in the slums and cared for the sick. On Oct. 7, 1950, she founded the Missionaries of Charity to give wholehearted free service to the poor in homes for the dying, shelter for orphans, care for lepers, and feeding and clothing the destitute. Her sisters serve in all parts of the world working for the "salvation and sanctification of the poorest of the poor." The Holy Eucharist is the strength for their mission to be "God's love in action" serving Jesus in the "distressing disguise of the poor." In 1979, Mother Teresa received the Nobel Peace Prize for her worldwide mission to the poor. Her work of bringing Jesus to the poor in the spirit of Mary has inspired numerous vocations in her order, and has made her an incarnation of the beatitudes of Jesus to channel God's love in the modern world.

The Beatitudes

Blessed are the poor in spirit, for the kingdom of heaven is theirs. Blessed are they who mourn, for they shall be comforted. Blessed are the meek, for they shall inherit the earth. Blessed are they who hunger and thirst for holiness, for they shall be satisfied. Blessed are the merciful, for they shall receive mercy. Blessed are the pure of heart, for they shall see God. Blessed are the peacemakers, for they shall be called the children of God. Blessed are they who are persecuted for the sake of truth, for the kingdom of heaven is theirs.

"When I was hungry, you gave Me to eat"

St. Nicholas

NICHOLAS was born at Patara, a province of Lycia, and became the Archbishop of Myra in Asia Minor. He is reported to have been taken a prisoner during the persecution of Emperor Diocletian, and later to have attended the Council of Nicaea in 325 which firmly opposed the Arian heresy. He is known to have raised three children to life after they were pickled in a tub of salt water. He is believed to have saved three young women from prostitution when, on three separate occasions, he threw a bag of gold in the window of their home to provide them with a dowry for marriage. These miracles and incidents of charity are said to have started the tradition of St. Nicholas, or Santa Claus, who gives gifts and presents, especially to children, at Christmas. Santa Claus is a secular symbol of a bishop. His staff, cap, suit as well as his sleigh, gifts and elves are reminders of a bishop's crozier, mitre and priestly vestments, and that he rules as a spiritual king who dispenses the treasury of God's grace through the assistance of his priests. St. Nicholas died in 350 and is one of the most popular saints in all of Christendom. He is the patron saint of children, sailors and Russia.

St. Nicholas, Bishop

O God, Who granted to Thy holy Bishop Nicholas the grace of numerous miracles, may we through his merits and prayers be delivered from the everlasting flames of hell. Through Christ our Lord. Amen.

Prayer for Children

O St. Nicholas, protect our children from bodily and spiritual harm. May the birth of Jesus fill their hearts with love and joy, that they will follow your spirit of charity and grow in their love for God. Amen.

Merry Christmas!

St. Paul Miki and Companions

PAUL MIKI was born in 1564 at Tokushima, Japan. His family converted to Christianity when he was around the age of four. He entered a Jesuit seminary in 1584 and joined them in 1586. He was an excellent defender and preacher of the Christian faith, converting many non-believers to the faith. During a persecution in 1596, Paul and twenty-five other Catholics were sentenced to be crucified in Nagasaki. On Feb. 5, 1597, as they were led to the hill of crucifixion, they sang the *Te Deum*. While hanging on his cross, Paul preached a sermon inviting the bystanders to live and die for Christ. He forgave his executioner and then he and his companions were each lanced twice by a soldier. Paul Miki and his companions were among the 200,000 Christians that were the fruit of the missionary efforts of St. Francis Xavier who brought Christianity to Japan in 1549. Paul and his companions were canonized by Pope Pius IX on June 8, 1862.

St. Paul Miki, Martyr

Almighty God, grant that we may be strengthened in Thy love and delivered from all adversity through the merits of Thy martyr Paul Miki and his companions that we may rejoice in their fellowship in the everlasting bliss of heaven. Through Christ our Lord. Amen.

The Salvation of the Lord

The salvation of the just is from the Lord. He is their protection in time of trouble. Be not emulous of those who do evil, nor envy them that work iniquity. For the just cried out, and the Lord heard them and delivered them from all their troubles. God saves the humble of spirit. Amen.

APOSTLE of ROME

St. Philip Neri

ST. PHILIP NERI was born in Florence, Italy in 1515. He worked for his uncle until he decided to live in poverty in Rome and educate children. In 1544, after he experienced an ecstasy of God's love that enlarged his heart, he devoted himself to the study of theology and works of charity. In 1548, he founded a religious community that became the Congregation of the Oratory. He was ordained in 1551 and through the apostolic labors of his oratory, the fervor for Christian life was enlivened amidst the corruption in Rome. He promoted the frequent reception of the sacraments and the need for solid catechetical formation in the Catholic faith. He was known to raise the dead to life and because of his great love for the Eucharist, he would spend up to three hours offering the Holy Sacrifice of the Mass. Philip was an advisor to popes and cardinals and the spiritual charm of his cheerful, gentle character inspired in others a true love for God. He died in 1595 and was canonized in 1622. He is called the "Second Apostle of Rome."

St. Philip Neri

O Lord, Who inflamed the heart of Thy Confessor Philip with the fire of Thy love and made him zealous in the conversion of souls, grant that by his prayers we may love Thee faithfully and serve Thee with a gentle spirit. We ask this in the name of Jesus Christ our Lord. Amen.

Prayer to St. Philip

O gentle lover of God, St. Philip Neri, we ask that through our worthy reception of the sacraments and our fidelity to the teachings of Christ, we may increase our love for God and convert others by our example. We ask this through Jesus Christ our Lord. Amen.

St. Philomena

PHILOMENA, POWERFUL WITH GOD, is a title she earned through the miraculous favors of her powerful intercession. In 1802, a tomb containing the bones, skull and a vial of blood from a young girl was discovered in the catacombs of St. Priscilla in Rome. The tomb was marked with three red tiles on which was written "Peace be with you, Philomena" and on which there was etched a lily, anchor and arrows to indicate that she was a virgin-martyr. The relics were brought to a shrine in Mugnano, Italy in 1805 and thereafter visiting pilgrims received miraculous blessings and favors. In 1837, Pope Gregory XVI called Philomena "the wonder worker" and declared her a saint. He named her "Patroness of the Living Rosary." The Curé of Ars, who was devoted to St. Philomena, credited her with the many miraculous events in his village. Pope Pius IX made her "Patroness of the Children of Mary." St. Philomena was raised to the altar of sanctity solely through her powerful intercession, since details of her life were unknown. She is known to grant requests for conversions, cures, the resolution of marriage difficulties and is a powerful advocate before God for even the smallest favor.

Prayer to St. Philomena

O faithful and glorious virgin-martyr, St. Philomena, wonder worker of many miraculous favors. You know the needs of poor sinners. Graciously obtain from God the favor I now bring before you *(make your request)*. Through the merits of your suffering in union with the cross of Jesus, I believe you will answer my prayer. Amen.

Prayer for Faith

Dear St. Philomena, ever solicitous of the need for faith in God, by your powerful intercession, assist the Church in converting sinners, returning the fallen away to the practice of the Catholic faith, giving families the courage to follow the laws of God and helping priests to remain faithful in their vocations. We ask this through Christ our Lord. Amen.

The Poor Souls in Purgatory

THE POOR SOULS IN PURGATORY are separated from the vision of God because they need to make satisfaction for the sins they committed during their lifetime on earth. They are suffering in fire worse than any earthly fire to expiate the temporal punishment due to their sins. The souls in purgatory are helpless and must rely on the prayers, good works and Masses offered on their behalf by the faithful in the Church on earth to relieve their suffering. It is a spiritual work of mercy and charity for the faithful on earth to pray for the poor souls, especially through the Holy Sacrifice of the Mass, which hastens their entrance into heaven. The poor souls are holy souls who will one day be perfectly purified to enter into the holy presence of God and who will not forget to pray for those who relieve their suffering. Through the worthy reception of the sacraments, penance, the patient bearing of suffering and the gaining of indulgences, the faithful can shorten or avoid time in purgatory. As members of the Body of Christ, the holy souls long for the glory of heaven that will unite them forever to the Bridegroom of their souls.

The Souls in Purgatory

O gentle Heart of Jesus, ever present in the Blessed Sacrament, ever consumed with burning love for the poor captive souls in purgatory, have mercy on them. Be not severe in Your judgments, but let some drops of Your Precious Blood fall upon the devouring flames. And, merciful Savior, send Your angels to conduct them to a place of refreshment, light and peace. Amen.

The Poor Souls

O Lord, the Creator and Redeemer of all the faithful, grant to the souls of Thy servants departed the remission of all their sins; that by the humble supplications of Thy Church, they may obtain the pardon which they have always desired of Thy Mercy. We ask this through Christ our Lord. Amen.

Lux aetérna lúceat eis

Pope John Paul II

POPE JOHN PAUL II, Karol Wojtyla, was born in Wadowice, Poland on May 18, 1920. Initially attracted to theatrical arts and poetry, he later studied in an underground seminary in Cracow and was ordained on Nov. 1, 1946. He received a doctorate in theology and was assigned to be an assistant pastor and chaplain. He became a professor of ethics and in 1958 was named an auxiliary bishop and in 1964 an archbishop. He attended Vatican Council II and contributed to *Gaudium et Spes*. In 1967, he was made a cardinal and served on the permanent council of the Bishop's Synod. Since his election to the Chair of Peter on Oct. 16, 1978, John Paul has travelled widely around the world bringing Christ's message of peace, reconciliation and truth. A prolific speaker and writer, he has proclaimed the transcendent dignity of the human person, upheld the teaching of *Humanae Vitae*, defended the irreplaceable role of the Christian family, reconfirmed Mary's exemplary presence in the life of the Church, and articulated the principles of morality. Under his reign, a Holy Year and Marian Year were celebrated, and a new code of canon law and a universal catechism were promulgated. He has courageously disciplined theologians and worked for an ecumenism that is faithful to Church doctrine. John Paul's apostolic mission is preparing the Church for a new evangelization to bring forth a culture of love and life and the glorification of God's holiness. On June 8, 1994 he said, "the man of the year 2000 must have Christ's Heart to know God and to know himself; he needs It to build the civilization of love."

Prayer to Mary

O Mary, Mother of Mercy, watch over all people, that the Cross of Christ may not be emptied of its power, that man may not stray from the path of the good or become blind to sin, but may put his hope ever more fully in God Who is "rich in mercy." May he carry out the good works prepared by God beforehand and so live completely "for the praise of His glory." Amen.

"The future of man passes by way of the family"

The Presentation of the Child Jesus

FORTY DAYS AFTER THE BIRTH OF JESUS, Mary and Joseph brought Him to the Temple in Jerusalem to consecrate Him to the Lord. They offered two turtledoves according to the law of Moses in gratitude for the deliverance of the Israelites in Egypt. The prophetess Anna and a holy and just man, the prophet Simeon, who prayed that before his death he would see the Messiah, were in the temple. Simeon recognized the Child in Mary's arms as the "anointed of the Lord." He took Him in his arms and proclaimed Him the Savior and Light of the nations, *"lumen ad revelatiónem géntium."* He prophesied that the Child was destined for the fall and rising of many in Israel, a sign of contradiction that would bring a sword of sorrow into Mary's Heart. Mary knew that Jesus was "the glorious King of the new Light," and she accepted God's will to bear the sorrow that would bring forth the salvation of souls. The feast of the Presentation, known as the Purification of Mary or Candlemas Day, is liturgically celebrated of Feb. 2 with a procession of lighted candles to signify that Jesus is the Light of the world. He entered the Temple of the Lord that we would find Him in the arms of Mary and offer ourselves to God with a pure heart.

The Presentation of the Lord

O Lord Jesus Christ, Who appeared among men in the substance of our flesh and was presented by Thy parents in the temple, and was recognized and received in the arms of the prophet Simeon and blessed by him, mercifully grant that, enlightened and taught by the grace of the Holy Spirit, we may truly acknowledge Thee and faithfully love Thee. Who with the Father and the Holy Spirit lives and reigns forever. Amen.

Queen of Heaven and Earth

MARY is Queen of heaven and earth and all creatures because she consented to be the Mother of the Incarnate Word. She became the Mother of the God-man, Who is the Lord and King of all things. From the moment of her Immaculate Conception, she surpassed all other creatures in the supernatural dignity of grace, virtue and glory which gave her the singular privilege of participating in her Son's work of salvation as His perfect disciple and collaborator. She shared in His victory over the dominion of Satan and sin and was assumed into heaven at the end of her life to become the Queen of His kingdom that has no end. Her royal rule is a superterrestial power of grace and love that leads souls to the kingdom of heaven. Mary exceeds all the angels and saints in the splendor of glory and is the highest creature in heaven next to the Blessed Trinity. As the first of the redeemed, she is a living and certain sign that those who follow her Son will receive the crown of everlasting life. Since the 4th century, the Church has honored Mary with the royal title of Queen and in 1954 Pope Pius XII established the feast of the Queenship of Mary.

Mary our Queen

We wish to exalt your Queenship and to recognize it as due to the sovereign excellence of your whole being, O dearest One, truly Mother of Him Who is King by right, by inheritance and by conquest. Reign, O Mother and Queen, by showing us the path of holiness and by guiding and assisting us that we may never stray from it. Amen.

The Queenship of Mary

Grant, we beg of You, O Lord, that we who honor the Blessed Virgin Mary, our Queen, may merit under her loving protection to attain peace on this earth and glory in heaven. Through Christ our Lord. Amen.

Queen of Mercy

Show us the kingdom of God.

St. Raphael and Tobias

RAPHAEL, an archangel who worships before the glory of God, was sent by God to cure the blindness of Tobit and give a husband to Sarah. Tobit was a just man who gave alms, fed the hungry, blessed God in all things and taught his son Tobias the ways of God. After burying a dead man one evening, Tobit was blinded by the droppings of sparrows. He became poor and told Tobias to go with a companion to recover his deposit of silver. Tobias found Raphael, known to him as Azarius. On the journey, Tobias caught a fish and Raphael told him to remove the heart, liver and gall for curative purposes. Raphael told Tobias about a kinswoman of his father, named Sarah. They visited Sarah's father and he agreed to the marriage even though she had seven husbands that were killed by a demon. On the wedding night, Tobias burned the heart and liver from the fish which drove away the demon and he and Sarah prayed for God's protection. When Sarah's father learned that God spared Tobias, he prepared a wedding feast. Raphael then recovered the silver and Tobias, Sarah and Raphael went to see Tobit who was overjoyed that they returned safely. After Tobias applied the gall to his father's eyes, Tobit could see again. Raphael refused any payment for his services and revealed to them his true identity. Tobit and his family then gave thanks to God, the King of the ages and Father forever.

St. Raphael

O God, Who gave St. Raphael the Archangel, the angelic physician of body and soul, to Thy humble servant Tobias as a companion on his journey, may he defend the sacrament of marriage from demonic powers and guide the faithful on the road to heaven where they will see Thy Face forever. Through Christ our Lord. Amen.

St. Rita of Cascia

ST. RITA was born near Spoletto, Italy in 1381. She desired to be a nun, but was married at the age of twelve in obedience to the plans of her parents. She became a faithful Catholic wife and mother and withstood the outrages and infidelities of her husband who eventually repented through her prayers. They were married eighteen years when he was killed. Her twin sons wanted to avenge their father's death, but Rita prayed they would not carry out their intention. A short time later, they died of an illness after receiving the Last Sacraments. As a widow, Rita attempted to enter the religious life several times, and in 1413 was finally admitted into an Augustinian convent at Cascia. She desired to participate in the sufferings of Christ and, in a mystical experience in 1441, she received a permanent wound from a thorn on a crucifix which caused her much suffering the rest of her life. She died in 1457 and her body has remained incorrupt. Many miracles have occurred at her tomb and her intercession has brought many back to the Church. She was canonized in 1900 and is a patroness of impossible cases.

St. Rita of Cascia

O God, Who gave to St. Rita the grace to partake of Thy Passion and to bear on her forehead a sacred wound from Thy crown of thorns, grant that, by her merits and prayers, we may learn to love our enemies and to have true contrition and sorrow for our sins. We ask this through Christ our Lord. Amen.

Prayer to St. Rita

O St. Rita, by your love of neighbor and devotion to the Passion of Jesus which purified your soul, obtain for me the grace to imitate your example of penance, perseverance and trust in Divine Providence that will convert sinners and defeat the spirit of enmity. We ask this through Jesus Christ our Lord. Amen.

Archbishop Fulton J. Sheen

FULTON J. SHEEN was born May 8, 1895 in El Paso, Illinois to Newton Sheen and Delia (Fulton) Sheen. He was baptized Peter, but later took his mother's maiden name. His father ran a hardware store and owned farm lands, where his sons milked cows, fed pigs and made hay. The family rosary was said every evening and priests visited their home frequently. He attended Catholic grade school in Peoria, was high school salutatorian and after college enrolled at the St. Paul Seminary in St. Paul, Minnesota. Ordained on Sept. 20, 1919, he went on to receive advanced degrees from Louvain and Rome. After a year of parish work, he joined the philosophy faculty at the Catholic University of America. In 1950, he became a national missions director and in 1951 was consecrated a bishop in Rome. He attended Vatican Council II and in 1966 was appointed bishop of Rochester, New York and named a titular Archbishop in 1969. An exceptionally gifted speaker and media apostle of God's word, who began each day with a Holy Hour, Archbishop Sheen reached millions in his more than twenty-five years of radio and television broadcasting. His numerous books, tapes, retreats and sermons inspired a Catholic fervor and won many converts. His deep love for God and the Church helped others to find the faith in Christ that made life worth living. He died in 1979.

For the Propagation of the Faith

O God, Who wills that all men may be saved and come to the knowledge of Thy Truth, we beg Thee to send forth many laborers into Thy harvest, that with the help of Thy grace they may boldly proclaim Thy word and glorify Thy Name before the nations so that all men may know Thee and Thy Son, Jesus Christ, Whom Thou has sent for the salvation of their souls. Amen.

St. Stephen

STEPHEN, meaning "crown," was a convert to Christianity in the first century and was ordained a deacon by the Apostles to care for the poor in Jerusalem. He was an excellent preacher, alive with the Holy Spirit in his defense of God's truth. Renowned for his virtue, he worked great miracles and signs and converted many to the Christian faith. He was accused of speaking contrary to the authority of God and Moses and had to defend himself before the officials in Jerusalem. His face looked like that of an angel when he spoke of Jesus, Whom he saw in the heavens at the right hand of God. The eloquent wisdom and testimony of his faith in Jesus angered his accusers and they dragged him outside the city where they stoned him to death. As he was dying, he prayed for the forgiveness of his executioners and said, "Lord Jesus, receive my spirit...Lord, lay not this sin to their charge." St. Stephen was the first martyr of the Church and is commemorated in the Canon of the Mass.

St. Stephen

O God, grant that we may learn to love our enemies as we celebrate the heavenly birthday of Thy holy servant Stephen who prayed for his persecutors to the Lord Jesus, Thy Son, Who lives and reigns with Thee in the unity of the Holy Spirit for ever and ever. Amen.

Words of St. Stephen

Moses performed wonders and signs in Egypt. Behold I see the heavens opened and Jesus standing at the right hand of the power of God. Lord Jesus, receive my spirit and lay not this sin to their charge.

"Blessed are they who follow the law of the Lord"

St. Teresa of Ávila

ST. TERESA OF JESUS was born on Mar. 28, 1515 in Ávila, Spain. At an early age she enjoyed reading the lives of the saints, and was devoted to Sts. Augustine and Mary Magdalen, and to St. Joseph who cured her of a crippling disease. After her mother died, she was educated at a convent, and then eventually decided in 1534 to enter the Carmelite convent of the Incarnation in Ávila. In 1562 she became the foundress of a convent dedicated to St. Joseph, and began a reform in the Carmelite order for more detachment, penance, silence and prayer. She founded sixteen convents, and with the help of St. John of the Cross, she formed the Discalced Carmelites. Her reform was recognized by Pope Gregory XIII. St. Teresa combined mystical contemplation with great practical accomplishments. She was a mystic who wrote several famous books about her union with God, and was an exceptional teacher of prayer, gifted with wise judgement and the grace of mystical marriage. She died on Oct. 4, 1582 and was canonized in 1622. St. Teresa was declared a Doctor of the Church by Pope Paul VI on Sept. 27, 1970. She is usually pictured with an angel piercing her heart.

St. Teresa, Virgin

Graciously hear us, O God our Savior, that as we rejoice in the glory of Thy Virgin, Teresa, so we may be fed with the food of her heavenly teaching, and grow in loving devotion for Thee. We ask this through Christ our Lord. Amen.

St. Teresa's Bookmark

Let nothing disturb you; nothing frighten you. All things are passing. God never changes. Patience obtains all things. Nothing is wanting to him who possesses God. God alone suffices.

The Glory of Truth

May God who favors truth be praised! May it please His Majesty that this all be for His honor and glory.

Blessed Teresa Benedicta

BLESSED SISTER TERESA BENEDICTA OF THE CROSS, known as Edith Stein, was born on Oct. 12, 1891 in a devout Jewish family at Breslau, Silesia. As a youth, she lost her faith in God and in her search for truth, she studied phenomenology and became a philosopher. After reading the autobiography of St. Teresa of Ávila, she decided to become a Catholic and was baptized on Jan. 1, 1922. Her conversion was an intellectual and spiritual union that recognized God as the essential foundation for all existence. She taught for eight years at a Dominican convent school and on Oct. 14, 1933 entered the Discalced Carmelite convent in Cologne, and then took the name Teresa Benedicta of the Cross. She desired to suffer with Christ in His redemptive work to "offer myself to the Heart of Jesus as sacrificial expiation for the sake of the world." During the Nazi persecution in Germany in 1938, she moved to the Carmel of Echt, Holland. In 1942, she and her sister were among the Catholics of Jewish descent that were arrested by the Nazis and sent to Auschwitz where they died in the gas chambers on Aug. 9, 1942. Her heroic love for Christ and the Jewish people led her to participate in the Passion of Christ that unites the soul to Truth itself. She was beatified on May 1, 1987.

The Truth of the Cross

Lord Jesus, on the Cross You are the power of God and the wisdom of God. Your Blood is the curtain by which we enter the Holiest of Holies and are cleansed of our sins, our eyes are opened to Your eternal light and our ears hear Your divine truth. Through the prayers of Blessed Teresa Benedicta, may we be nourished by Your Body and Blood and become one with Your Flesh and Blood that we may offer ourselves to Your holy will. Amen.

St. Thomas Aquinas

ST. THOMAS AQUINAS, the Angelic Doctor, was born near Aquino, Italy in 1225. At age five, he was educated at Monte Cassino. In 1243, he joined the Dominicans, but his family disagreed, holding him captive for two years. But he prevailed, and rejoined the order in 1245. He studied under St. Albert the Great, overcame the name "dumb ox," and became his assistant. He was ordained and then became a master of theology, frequently lecturing in Paris and Rome. He was adept in refuting error and defending Catholic truth. His eloquence and precise exposition demonstrated the intellectual coherence of Divine Revelation. He achieved a synthesis between faith and reason and wrote many scholarly works, among them the *Summa Theologiae*, his monumental masterpiece. He was an outstanding preacher, teacher and intellectual genius whose theological work was founded upon his love for the immutable truths revealed by God. Numerous pontiffs recognized the essence of his thought, and it became official Church teaching. He was a man of great humility who wrote excellent hymns and prayers. He died on Mar. 7, 1274 on his way to the Second Council of Lyons. He was canonized in 1323 and declared a Doctor of the Church in 1567. Pope Leo XIII made him patron of Catholic schools. He once said, "the Church of Peter flourishes in faith and is immune from error." St. Thomas was a theological sun that nourished the world with the brilliance of Divine Truth.

St. Thomas, Doctor

O God, Who gave glory to the Church with the inspired teaching of St. Thomas, Your holy Confessor, and rendered it fruitful by his holy deeds, grant that we may understand what he taught and follow his good example. Through Christ our Lord. Amen.

O Sacrum Convivium

O Sacred Banquet wherein Christ is received; the memory of His Passion is renewed, the mind is filled with grace, and the pledge of future glory is given unto us. Amen.

Tu Rex Gloriae, Christe.

"I am willing to accept any child who would be aborted and to give that child to a married couple who will love the child and be loved by the child."

Mother Teresa of Calcutta

The Unborn Child

MOTHER TERESA OF CALCUTTA, INDIA, foundress of the Missionaries of Charity, spoke to the National Prayer Breakfast attended by representatives from over one hundred nations in Washington, D.C. on Feb. 3, 1994. In her address, she said, "the greatest destroyer of peace today is abortion because it is a war against the child, a direct killing of the innocent child." "By Abortion, the mother does not learn to love, but kills her own child to solve her problems." The "unborn child has been carved in the hand of God from conception and is called by God to love and to be loved, not only now in this life, but forever." When "living love is destroyed by contraception, abortion easily follows…which brings a people to be spiritually poor." *"I am willing to accept any child who would be aborted"* and "I will never give a child to a couple who have done something not to have a child." "Any country that accepts abortion is not teaching its people to love, but to use violence to get what they want." By loving others "America can become…a sign of care for the weakest of the weak, the unborn child." Through the patronage of St. Joseph and Our Lady of Guadalupe, the mission and destiny of the child revealed in the Child Jesus is realized in the prophetic voice of Mother Teresa that "the child is God's gift to the family."

Prayer for the Unborn Child

Heavenly Father, Creator of human life, watch over the unborn child that You made in Your image and likeness. Help all families to welcome Your gift of the child who is destined for the glory of eternal life. May the nations of the world protect Your precious gift of unborn human life from its very beginning, and safeguard the Christian family through which true peace is found in society. Amen.

"Love begins at home in the family"

St. Vincent de Paul

VINCENT DE PAUL was born on Apr. 24, 1580 in Pouy, France. He was a gifted student and was ordained in 1600 at age twenty. He was captured by pirates during a sea voyage and sold into slavery in Algeria. He was freed after he converted one of his slave masters. He studied in Rome and later did parish missions in France. He became a follower of St. Francis de Sales and then ministered to the destitute and the poor. He founded the Congregation of the Mission and the Sisters of Charity, dedicated to alleviating human suffering and poverty. St. Vincent also established hospitals, orphanages and sheltered victims of war and provided refuge for Christian slaves. He opened a seminary and did spiritual writing. He was known for his deeds of charity through his relief organizations that were open to all classes of people. He was a spiritual father of orphans and lived "to plant the Gospel-spirit of charity, humility, meekness and simplicity in the hearts of all Christians." He died on Sept. 27, 1660 and was canonized in 1737. He is the patron of charitable societies and his work continues in organizations such as the St. Vincent de Paul Society.

Prayer to St. Vincent de Paul

O glorious St. Vincent, heavenly patron of charitable societies and spiritual father of those in misery, while on earth you extended a kindly hand to the needy. Through your merciful intercession, obtain help for the destitute, relief for the abandoned, solace for the unfortunate, comfort for the sick and the grace of preaching the Gospel to the poor. May your example of charity encourage priests to work for the salvation of all souls that the love of Christ may be known to all people. We ask this through Christ our Lord. Amen.